I0540531

# EPIC LOVE STORIES
# OF THE BIBLE

By Karajah Yashar

PASSED
OVER
PRESS

TRUTH BEYOND TRADITION

Orlando, FL

# Epic Love Stories
# of the Bible

ISBN: 978-1-962691-58-1
First Edition: February 2026

# Acknowledgment

This book is written for all believers who are striving to pattern their relationships after godly example. It is for those who understand that love is more than emotion—it is obedience, sacrifice, patience, and covenant. These pages are offered to readers who desire to love as God designed, whether in marriage, family, or community, and who recognize that Scripture provides both instruction and correction for every season of relationship.

This work also honors those who are still learning, healing, and growing. The love stories found in the Bible are not flawless, and neither are we. They reveal both faithfulness and failure, showing us how God meets people where they are and leads them toward something better. May these stories encourage perseverance, humility, and trust in God's timing, even when relationships feel complicated or incomplete.

Above all, this book is an offering to those committed to walking in truth. May it strengthen your resolve to live out love as a lifestyle, not a label—rooted in God's commandments, guided by His wisdom, and shaped by His enduring grace.

# Table of Contents

## Introduction

The Bible is often approached as a book of laws, prophecies, and moral instruction—and it is all of those things. But beneath every commandment and covenant runs a deeper current: love. Not the fragile, sentimental love modern culture celebrates, but a love that endures betrayal, survives silence, withstands waiting, and remains faithful when circumstances collapse. *Epic Love Stories of the Bible* invites you to encounter that current—to see Scripture not as a distant record of ancient lives, but as a living testimony of how love was designed to work.

These are not fairy tales. They are not sanitized romances or idealized unions untouched by conflict. The love stories of the Bible are epic precisely because they are costly. They involve sacrifice, obedience, patience, and often pain. They unfold in tents and prisons, in palaces and fields, under threat of death and under the weight of unanswered prayers. And yet, through all of it, love remains purposeful. It builds families, preserves nations, restores the broken, and reveals the heart of God Himself.

From Adam and Eve, learning love in innocence and failure, to Ruth and Boaz, discovering redemption through loyalty and integrity, Scripture shows us that love is never accidental. It is formative. Each relationship becomes a blueprint—either for what strengthens covenant or for what fractures it. Some stories end in unity. Others end in warning. All of them teach.

This book gathers those stories not to romanticize the past, but to illuminate the present. We live in a time that speaks endlessly about love yet struggles to define it. Love is treated as emotion rather than responsibility, attraction rather than alignment, and self-fulfillment rather than covenant. The biblical narratives stand in stark contrast. Here, love is not measured by how it feels in the moment, but by what it is willing to endure for the sake of purpose.

In these pages, you will meet men and women who waited years for one another, who honored boundaries in the face of desire, who protected one another at great personal risk, and who sometimes failed—deeply. You will also meet relationships undone by pride, passivity, lust, and power. Scripture does not hide these fractures. Instead, it uses them as instruction. Love that is not guarded can be corrupted. Love that is not aligned with God can be weaponized. And love that refuses correction can destroy both people and purpose.

Yet woven throughout these stories is a greater revelation: God is not merely observing human love—He is shaping it. He steps into marriages, corrects course, redeems failures, and restores hope where love seems lost. The ultimate love story, Christ and the Church, stands as the crown of them all—a love defined not by romance, but by sacrifice; not by convenience, but by covenant. It is from this divine pattern that all healthy love flows.

*Epic Love Stories of the Bible* is written for readers who sense that love must be more than what the world is offering. It is for those who are married, waiting, healing, or rebuilding. It is for those who want to understand how love is meant to function—not just between two people, but within families, communities, and a holy nation set apart for God's purposes.

Each story in this book is explored not only for what happened, but for what it teaches. You will see how patience shapes love, how obedience protects it, how silence can wound it, and how repentance can restore it. You will encounter love that waited fourteen years, love that crossed ethnic and cultural boundaries, love that endured barrenness and loss, love that failed through pride, and love that redeemed through faithfulness.

These stories matter because they are not finished. They are still being lived out—every time a husband chooses sacrifice over self-interest, every time a wife chooses trust over fear, every time loyalty triumphs over convenience, and every time God's ways are chosen over cultural pressure. The Bible's love stories are epic not because they are ancient, but because they are eternal.

As you enter this book, you are not merely reading history. You are stepping into mirrors. Somewhere in these pages, you will recognize your own questions, struggles, hopes, and callings. And perhaps, through these stories, you will rediscover what love was always meant to be: purposeful, covenantal, and anchored in God.

This is not a book about perfect people. It is a book about faithful love.

# 1

# Adam and Eve

*Adam and Eve: The First Love and the Blueprint of All Relationships*

Before there were cities and ceremonies, before laws and love songs, there was a garden. And in that garden, love was not learned—it was *given*. Adam and Eve stand at the beginning of every human relationship not because they were perfect, but because they were first. Their story is the foundation upon which all love stories rise, fracture, repair, and try again. It is the blueprint, not because it shows us how love never fails, but because it shows us what love was meant to be *before fear entered the room*.

Adam was not lonely because he lacked people; he was lonely because he lacked reflection. The animals passed before him, each with a partner, each complete in their own kind, yet none mirrored his essence. God's response was not a lecture or a distraction—it was intimacy. Eve was formed from Adam's side, not from his head to rule him, nor from his feet to be trampled by him, but from his rib, close to his heart. From the very beginning, love was designed to be mutual, equal in value, distinct in function, and unified in purpose.

When Adam first saw Eve, his response was poetry before poetry existed. "Bone of my bones, and flesh of my flesh." This was recognition, not possession. He did not name her to control her, but to acknowledge kinship. She was not a helper because she was lesser, but because love itself requires partnership. In this, we see the original blueprint of relationship: *oneness without erasure*. Two people, whole on their own, choosing to walk in harmony.

In the garden, love was uncomplicated. There was no shame in nakedness, no fear of being seen fully. Emotional safety existed before emotional language did. Adam and Eve lived in a world where communication was unguarded, affection was natural, and trust flowed freely. They walked with God together, not hiding, not blaming, not competing. This is the foundation of all healthy relationships: shared purpose, shared presence, and shared accountability before something greater than self.

But love, even in its purest form, was given a choice.

The mistake Adam and Eve made was not simply eating fruit—it was *breaking alignment*. Eve listened to a voice that questioned God's intention, and Adam listened to silence when he should have spoken. The serpent did not attack love directly; it attacked trust. It introduced suspicion where security once lived. "Did God really say?" That question still echoes through marriages, friendships, and families today. Doubt enters quietly, often disguised as independence or curiosity, and once trust is fractured, intimacy soon follows.

Eve acted independently of shared counsel, and Adam abdicated leadership through passivity. This is the relational fracture that repeats itself across generations. One partner moves ahead without covering, the other withdraws instead of protecting. Love becomes unbalanced—not because one is evil and the other is innocent, but because communication breaks down. When Adam ate, it was not out of deception, but out of misplaced loyalty. He chose Eve over God instead of choosing God *for* Eve. And in that moment, love lost its center.

The immediate consequence was not punishment—it was shame. They saw themselves differently, and then they saw each other differently. Nakedness, once a symbol of trust, became a source of fear. They covered themselves, not because their bodies changed, but because vulnerability now felt dangerous. This is the second great lesson in the blueprint of relationships: when spiritual alignment is broken, emotional distance is never far behind.

Then came blame—the most common language of broken love. Adam pointed to Eve. Eve pointed to the serpent. No one took responsibility without deflection. Love that once said "we" now said "me." This is where relationships still fall apart today. Accountability is replaced with accusation. Healing is delayed by pride. And yet, even here, God did not abandon them.

God sought them out. "Where are you?" Not because He lacked information, but because love always invites confession before correction. Even in failure, the blueprint remains clear: relationships survive not by perfection, but by honesty and repentance. God covered Adam and Eve Himself, clothing them with care even as consequences followed. Love did not disappear; it transformed.

Adam and Eve's story teaches us that relationships were never meant to exist apart from God. When love loses its spiritual anchor, it becomes fragile, fearful, and self-protective. But when love remains rooted in truth, humility, and shared responsibility, it becomes resilient—even after failure.

They were removed from the garden, but not from each other. They faced hardship together. They built family together. They lived with regret, but also with hope. Their love endured because it learned. And that is the final truth of their story: the blueprint was not destroyed—it was tested.

Every relationship since Adam and Eve has followed this same pattern: connection, choice, conflict, and either collapse or covenant renewal. Their story reminds us that love begins with unity, is sustained by obedience and communication, and is restored through accountability and grace.

Adam and Eve were not just the first couple. They were the first lesson. And every love story since has been answering the same question they faced in the garden: *Will we walk together in truth, or hide from one another in fear?*

That choice—then and now—still defines love.

---------------------------------------------------

## Adam and Even in the Modern World

If Adam and Eve were suddenly placed into the modern world, they would not be strangers to its technology as much as they would be strangers to its *noise*. Screens would not confuse them nearly as much as the constant pull for attention, comparison, and self-definition. In the garden, identity was received, not curated. Adam knew who he was because God spoke it, and Eve knew who she was because she was seen and valued without needing validation from anyone else. In a modern world obsessed with self-branding, Adam and Eve would struggle most with the pressure to perform rather than simply *be*.

Their relationship, however, would stand out. They would likely confuse people with how little they hide from one another. In a culture that guards vulnerability and monetizes intimacy, their openness would feel radical. They would not need couples therapy to learn how to communicate because communication was their default. Yet they would quickly feel the strain of a world that normalizes secrecy. Social media would test them—not because they would seek attention, but because comparison is the modern serpent, always whispering that what you have is not enough. Eve, especially, might feel the pressure of unrealistic ideals of beauty and success, while Adam might feel the weight of providing in a system that defines worth by productivity rather than presence.

The same ancient mistakes would likely reappear, just dressed differently. Eve might still be tempted to seek knowledge or empowerment apart from shared counsel, not through forbidden fruit, but through voices that promise independence without accountability. Adam might still struggle with passivity—not by silence in a garden, but by emotional withdrawal, overwork, or distraction. Their challenge in the modern world would not be temptation itself, but *disconnection*—from God, from each other, and from the stillness that once defined their life.

Yet Adam and Eve would also bring something the modern world is desperate for: clarity. They would remind people that partnership is not competition, that difference is not inequality, and that love thrives best when rooted in shared purpose rather than personal ambition. They would resist the pressure to make their relationship a public spectacle. Their love would be quiet, inconvenient, and countercultural— choosing faithfulness over novelty, presence over performance, and restoration over replacement.

In time, Adam and Eve would adapt, but not without cost. They would learn boundaries in a world without them. They would relearn trust in a culture that profits from doubt. And perhaps most importantly, they would show that even in a modern world fractured by fear and division, the original design for love—unity, responsibility, and humility—still works when people are willing to walk in it.

# 2

# Abraham and Sarah

*Love, Legacy, and Grace*

Long before love was romanticized, before partnership became a negotiation of power, there was Abraham and Sarah—two people bound not by ease, but by calling. Their love story is not remembered for passion or poetry, but for endurance. It is the story of a man and a woman who walked together through uncertainty, barrenness, fear, and faith, learning—often the hard way—how mutual respect does not mean sameness, and unity does not require identical roles.

When God first spoke to Abram, Sarai was already part of the promise, even before her name was spoken aloud. She was not consulted because she was invisible, but because covenant in that age moved through headship. Yet Sarai was never portrayed as silent, weak, or inconsequential. From the very beginning, their relationship reveals a delicate balance: Abraham carried the mantle of leadership and obedience to God's voice, while Sarah carried discernment, influence, and the emotional weight of the promise. Their love was not equal in function, but it was equal in value.

Sarah followed Abraham away from everything familiar—her land, her people, her security—into the unknown. That alone speaks volumes. Love, for her, was not passive agreement; it was active sacrifice. She trusted Abraham's ability to hear God even when the promise seemed to mock her reality. Year after year, she lived with the quiet ache of barrenness in a culture that measured a woman's worth by her womb. Still, she stayed. Still, she walked beside him. This is the first lesson of their love: *mutual respect is often expressed through trust in another's assignment, even when it costs you personally*.

Abraham, for his part, honored Sarah in ways that were subtle but significant. Scripture records that he listened to her voice, valued her counsel, and never treated her as disposable— even when fear tempted him to do otherwise. And fear did tempt him. Twice, Abraham failed Sarah by presenting her as his sister rather than his wife, choosing self-preservation over protection. These moments reveal one of the central mistakes in their relationship: Abraham struggled, at times, to fully cover Sarah when his own life felt threatened.

Yet even in this failure, something profound is revealed. God intervened on Sarah's behalf. Not Abraham. Not Pharaoh. Not kings or customs. God Himself protected her. This shows that while human relationships may falter, divine covenant does not. Abraham's mistake did not erase his calling, but it did expose a flaw many relationships still face today—when leadership is driven by fear rather than faith, those under its care are put at risk.

Sarah's mistake came later, born not from fear of danger, but fear of delay. The promise had been spoken, but time kept moving. Her body aged. Hope grew thin. And so Sarah did what many do when waiting becomes unbearable—she tried to help God. Offering Hagar to Abraham was not rebellion; it was desperation. In her mind, she was still supporting the promise, still honoring Abraham's role as patriarch. But she stepped outside her role by forcing fulfillment instead of trusting timing.

This decision fractured peace in their household. Hagar conceived, Sarah felt dishonored, and Abraham retreated into passivity, telling Sarah to handle the consequences herself. This reveals their second relational failure: *when pressure mounts, both partners momentarily abandoned their responsibilities*. Sarah acted outside her lane, and Abraham refused to lead decisively within his.

Yet even here, mutual respect did not disappear—it evolved. When conflict arose, Abraham still listened to Sarah. And later, when Sarah demanded Hagar and Ishmael be sent away, God told Abraham plainly: "Listen to Sarah." This moment is critical. It shows that respect in relationships is not static. Leadership does not mean unilateral decision-making, and submission does not mean silence. God affirmed Sarah's discernment, even after her earlier misstep, reinforcing that her voice mattered in shaping the family's future.

Perhaps the most tender moment in their love story comes not in youth, but in old age. When God declares that Sarah will bear a son, she laughs—not out of mockery, but disbelief shaped by disappointment. God does not rebuke her harshly. Instead, He names the child Isaac—laughter. This is divine compassion at work. God honors Sarah's emotional journey, turning her doubt into joy rather than shame.

Abraham never shames Sarah for her laughter. He never diminishes her because of her past mistake. When Isaac is finally born, it is not Abraham's triumph alone—it is Sarah's vindication. She names her joy openly, reclaiming her story. Their love matures here, no longer rooted in expectation, but in fulfillment that only God could bring.

Abraham and Sarah teach us that strong relationships are not built on identical roles, but on *honored distinctions*. Abraham led spiritually and externally. Sarah governed internally and relationally. When each stayed aligned with God and respected the other's function, peace followed. When fear or impatience disrupted that balance, conflict emerged.

Yet their story also teaches grace. Mistakes did not cancel the promise. Failures did not negate love. Growth came through humility, correction, and time. Their relationship survived not because they were flawless, but because they remained committed—to God, to each other, and to the process of becoming.

In the end, Abraham buried Sarah with honor, purchasing land to lay her to rest—a final act of respect that echoed a lifetime of partnership. She was not just his wife. She was his co-heir, his journey companion, his equal in promise, though different in role.

Their love story reminds us that healthy relationships are not about competing for position, but completing purpose. When roles are honored, voices respected, and God remains at the center, love does not merely survive—it leaves a legacy.

And that, perhaps, is the greatest love story of all.

## Abraham and Sarah in the Modern World

If Abraham and Sarah were living in the modern world, they would be the kind of couple people quietly admire but openly question. Their lives would not make sense on paper. Moving without guarantees, trusting a promise that had no timeline, and building a future around faith rather than data would feel reckless in an age obsessed with certainty. Yet it is precisely this tension that would define how they navigate the modern world—steadily, imperfectly, and with a kind of resilience that cannot be taught in self-help books.

Abraham would likely be viewed as a visionary—someone always talking about purpose, calling, and destiny. He would feel out of place in systems that demand immediate results and measurable success. His greatest struggle would be remaining faithful to a long-term promise in a culture that rewards short-term wins. Sarah, on the other hand, would feel the weight of comparison more acutely. In a world that measures a woman's worth by achievement, appearance, or motherhood, her long season of waiting would be amplified by constant reminders of what she did not yet have. Social media, baby announcements, and cultural timelines would test her patience in ways ancient tents never could.

Their relationship would still reveal the beauty—and the strain—of differing roles. Abraham would carry vision and direction, often moving ahead with confidence that Sarah would need time to process emotionally. Sarah would carry discernment and realism, asking the questions Abraham sometimes rushed past. In a healthy season, this balance would ground them. In moments of fear, it would divide them. Abraham might still struggle with protecting Sarah fully when his own security feels threatened—choosing caution or silence instead of bold advocacy. Sarah might still feel tempted to take control when waiting becomes unbearable, seeking solutions that make sense logically but bypass trust.

Yet what would set them apart in the modern world is their willingness to grow. Sarah's laughter—once rooted in disbelief—would eventually turn into a testimony. Abraham's faith—once marked by fear—would mature into steadiness. They would likely attend counseling not because their marriage was failing, but because they believed in alignment. They would learn to name their fears rather than act them out. And over time, their story would become one of hope for couples navigating delayed dreams and unanswered prayers.

Abraham and Sarah would remind the modern world that love does not require perfection, only perseverance. They would show that waiting does not mean being forgotten, and that roles in a relationship are not about power, but partnership. Their lives would still be marked by promise fulfilled late, joy arriving after doubt, and love strengthened—not weakened—by time.

# 3

# Isaac and Rebekah

*Love Born of Prayer, Shaped by Obedience, and Anchored in Comfort*

Some love stories begin with attraction. Others begin with longing. The love story of Isaac and Rebekah begins with *absence*—a quiet space left behind by loss, prayer, and trust in a God who arranges meetings long before hearts recognize one another. Their union is not rushed or reckless. It is not loud. It is steady, reverent, and deeply rooted in obedience. In a world that often mistakes passion for permanence, Isaac and

Rebekah remind us that love can be *built*, and that sometimes the most enduring bonds are the ones God assembles piece by piece.

Isaac first enters the story not as a man searching for love, but as a son carrying grief. His mother Sarah, the laughter of his childhood and the warmth of his home, has died. Scripture does not linger on his mourning, but the silence speaks volumes. Isaac is a quiet man by nature—meditative, inward, reflective. Where Abraham was bold and public in faith, Isaac's faith lived in stillness. He had watched his father trust God with impossible promises, had felt the weight of the altar on Mount Moriah, and now lived in the shadow of a great legacy with an empty place beside him where his mother once stood.

Abraham, aware of both the promise and the pain, takes responsibility not only for Isaac's future, but for his healing. He does not leave love to chance. He sends his servant with a prayerful mission—not simply to find a wife, but to find the *right* woman, one aligned with covenant, character, and calling. This is the first quiet truth in Isaac and Rebekah's story: love is safest when it is covered in prayer before it is carried by emotion.

Rebekah enters the narrative not adorned in titles or anticipation, but in motion. She is drawing water—doing ordinary work with uncommon diligence. When the servant prays for a sign, Rebekah answers it not with words, but with action. She offers water not only to the man, but to his camels, an act requiring strength, patience, and generosity. This is no small gesture. It is labor-intensive kindness, the kind that reveals character before intention is known. Rebekah does not know she is being watched by destiny. She is simply being herself.

When the servant explains why he has come, Rebekah listens. And when the moment comes to decide, she does something remarkable. She chooses willingly. No coercion. No delay. She leaves her family, her familiarity, her past, and steps into a future she cannot fully see. Her "I will go" echoes Sarah's earlier journey, but with a youthful courage that feels less burdened by doubt. Rebekah's obedience is not naive; it is brave. She trusts that the God who orchestrated the meeting will also sustain the marriage.

Isaac meets Rebekah not in a marketplace or at a celebration, but in a field—meditating, praying, breathing through his grief. When he lifts his eyes and sees her approaching, the moment is quiet but profound. There is no rush to touch, no flood of words. Rebekah veils herself, honoring the sanctity of the encounter. Isaac receives her not as a conquest, but as a gift. And Scripture says something tender and rare: *he loved her*.

This love is not described as sudden passion, but as something that grows from presence and purpose. Rebekah is brought into Sarah's tent, and in that sacred space, something begins to heal. Isaac is comforted after his mother's death. This detail is crucial. Rebekah does not replace Sarah, but she brings stability where there had been sorrow. Love, here, becomes restorative. It does not erase grief; it helps carry it.

Their marriage teaches us that love can be a balm. That partnership can provide emotional grounding when life has fractured us. Isaac's affection for Rebekah is deep, steady, and loyal. He does not collect wives. He does not wander. He cleaves to her, honoring the covenant of one flesh in a way that feels intentional and rare even within Scripture.

Yet their love story is not without struggle. Like Abraham and Sarah, Isaac and Rebekah face barrenness. The promise seems to stall again, as though waiting tests every generation. But unlike Sarah's earlier impatience, Isaac responds differently. He prays. He intercedes for his wife. This marks a quiet maturation in covenant relationships: Isaac learns from the past and chooses patience over panic. God hears him, and Rebekah conceives.

Rebekah, however, carries her own burden. The pregnancy is difficult, the children within her struggling violently. Confused and afraid, she does not turn inward—she inquires of the Lord. God answers her directly, honoring her spiritual agency. She learns that two nations wrestle within her womb, and that the future will not be simple. Love, even in obedience, does not guarantee ease.

Later, their relationship strains under favoritism. Isaac loves Esau. Rebekah loves Jacob. This division introduces tension into the household and eventually leads to deception. Rebekah, attempting to secure the promise she knows God has spoken, orchestrates a plan that deceives Isaac. This is her mistake—not born of malice, but of fear that God's word might fail without her intervention.

Isaac, on the other hand, struggles with discernment in his old age, guided more by appetite than insight. Both falter. Love bends under pressure. Yet even here, God's purpose moves forward, reminding us that divine plans are not undone by human weakness.

What remains remarkable is that Scripture never speaks of Isaac abandoning Rebekah, nor Rebekah withdrawing her loyalty. Their marriage endures. It stabilizes the lineage. It becomes a bridge between Abraham's bold beginnings and Jacob's complicated future.

Isaac and Rebekah show us a love shaped by prayer, sustained by obedience, and refined by time. Their story reminds us that love does not have to be dramatic to be powerful. Sometimes it is found in fields, in tents, in whispered prayers, and in the quiet comfort of knowing you are not alone.

Their union teaches us that when love is divinely arranged, it does more than satisfy desire—it brings healing, steadiness, and continuity. It anchors the heart after loss and provides a place to stand when the future feels uncertain.

In Isaac and Rebekah, we see that love, when rooted in God, becomes more than romance. It becomes refuge.

---------------------------------------------------------

## Isaac and Rebekah in the Modern World

If Isaac and Rebekah were living in the modern world, they would likely be the couple people describe as "quiet but solid." They would not be flashy, oversharing, or constantly redefining their relationship online. Instead, their strength would be found in consistency, prayer, and emotional steadiness—qualities often overlooked in a culture that celebrates intensity over endurance. Their love, formed through intention rather than impulse, would feel almost old-fashioned in a world that prefers immediacy.

Isaac, still shaped by early trauma and loss, would be a reflective man in a fast-moving society. He would struggle with environments that reward constant noise and visibility. Yet his contemplative nature would make him emotionally present in ways many modern men are not taught to be. He would value routine, spiritual grounding, and safe spaces—perhaps drawn to counseling, journaling, or quiet faith communities. Rebekah, by contrast, would be expressive, proactive, and socially aware. She would thrive in connection, quick to respond to needs and comfortable stepping into responsibility when necessary.

Their relationship would benefit from shared values and clear boundaries. Isaac would not chase multiple options or treat commitment casually, and Rebekah would respect the slow, deliberate pace of his love. In a dating culture defined by swiping and testing, they would likely meet through community—faith spaces, family connections, or service— and approach marriage with seriousness. Their courtship would be intentional, protected, and prayer-centered, resisting pressure to rush intimacy.

Their challenges, however, would mirror ancient ones in modern forms. Rebekah might still feel compelled to manage outcomes when uncertainty lingers, especially in seasons of waiting—whether for children, stability, or clarity. Isaac might still struggle with passivity during conflict, preferring peace over confrontation. In a modern household, this could show up as avoidance of difficult conversations or deferring decisions too long. Without care, these tendencies could create imbalance, with Rebekah over-functioning and Isaac under-engaging.

Yet their greatest strength would be their capacity for healing. Isaac's love would provide Rebekah with emotional safety, while Rebekah's initiative would help Isaac move forward when grief or hesitation slows him down. Together, they would model a relationship where love does not replace pain, but helps carry it. Their home would feel grounded, steady, and spiritually anchored—a place where people feel calm simply by entering.

In a modern world marked by instability and relational burnout, Isaac and Rebekah would quietly succeed—not because their marriage is perfect, but because it is intentional. They would remind others that love built on prayer, patience, and mutual respect still works, even now.

# 4

# Jacob and Rachel

*Love That Waited, Worked, and
Withstood the Long Road*

Some love stories are sudden sparks. Others are slow burns, forged through time, labor, and restraint. The love story of Jacob and Rachel belongs to the second kind—the kind that teaches patience not as passivity, but as devotion in motion. It is a story where desire is disciplined, longing is honorable, and love proves itself not by what it takes, but by what it is willing to wait for.

Jacob arrived in Haran tired, uncertain, and running from the consequences of his own deception. He had taken his brother's blessing and fled, carrying both promise and guilt on his back. When he reached the well and saw Rachel for the first time, Scripture tells us that something immediate stirred in him. She was beautiful, yes—but more than that, she represented rest. She was a glimpse of tenderness in a life shaped by striving. Jacob rolled away the stone from the well with a strength fueled by more than muscle. It was the strength of hope.

Yet what is striking about their story is not the intensity of Jacob's attraction, but the discipline of his response. In a culture where power often dictated access, Jacob did not take Rachel. He honored process. He spoke with her father. He agreed to work. Love, here, submits itself to order. Desire bows to covenant. There is no premarital intimacy recorded, no secret taking of what had not yet been given. Jacob's love waited, and in that waiting, it matured.

Laban, Rachel's father, was a man who recognized devotion when he saw it—and also a man willing to exploit it. When Jacob offered seven years of labor for Rachel's hand, it was an extravagant commitment. Seven years is a lifetime when you are young and in love. But Scripture tells us something extraordinary: "They seemed unto him but a few days, for the love he had to her." This was not infatuation. This was perseverance fueled by purpose. Jacob's love was not weakened by delay; it was deepened by it.

Rachel, meanwhile, lived in the quiet tension of being chosen yet unavailable. She was loved openly, but not yet possessed. There is dignity in her waiting as well. She does not seduce Jacob into shortcuts. She does not rebel against her father's authority. Her silence is not weakness—it is trust. Together, they model a truth often forgotten: restraint is not the enemy of romance; it is its safeguard.

But love that waits is still tested.

When the wedding night arrived and Jacob was deceived into marrying Leah instead, the betrayal cut deeply. Jacob's anger was real, but it also revealed a flaw—his tunnel vision. He loved Rachel so fiercely that he failed to see Leah at all. His devotion to one became neglect of another. This is one of the great mistakes in Jacob's love story: love, when narrowly focused, can become unjust.

Laban's deception created a household built on imbalance. Jacob married Rachel a week later, agreeing to seven more years of labor. Fourteen years of work. Fourteen years of patience. Fourteen years of showing love not through words, but through endurance. Jacob did not abandon Rachel when the road grew longer than promised. He stayed. He worked. He paid the cost.

Yet the marriage was not without strain. Rachel, loved deeply, struggled with barrenness. Leah, less loved, bore children easily. This imbalance exposed the wounds of comparison and competition. Rachel's mistake was allowing her worth to become entangled with her womb. In her pain, she cried out to Jacob in desperation, demanding children as proof of love. Jacob, wounded and overwhelmed, responded harshly, momentarily forgetting compassion.

Here we see another truth: even patient love can falter under unfulfilled longing. Rachel's jealousy and Leah's insecurity turned sisterhood into rivalry. Jacob, instead of correcting the imbalance, often tolerated it. His failure to emotionally shepherd both wives allowed resentment to grow. Love that had once been pure became complicated by favoritism.

And yet, patience continued to shape the story.

Rachel eventually bore Joseph, a child born not of striving, but of divine timing. Her joy was not loud—it was relieved. Jacob's love for Rachel never wavered, but it matured. It became protective, tender, and deeply loyal. When Rachel later died giving birth to Benjamin, Jacob's grief marked him permanently. He did not replace her. He carried her memory like a scar and a song all at once.

Jacob buried Rachel with honor, naming the place of her rest. Even in death, she remained distinct in his heart. His love had endured deception, delay, disappointment, and death itself. It was never easy—but it was faithful.

The love story of Jacob and Rachel teaches us that patience is not waiting without effort. It is waiting *with faithfulness*. Jacob worked. Rachel trusted. Together, they honored boundaries, endured hardship, and paid the price love required. Their mistakes remind us that love must be balanced with wisdom, empathy, and justice. Passion without awareness can wound others. Favor without responsibility can fracture families.

But at its core, their story is a testament to sacrificial love— love that waits, works, and withstands time. Love that refuses shortcuts. Love that understands that what is worth having is worth waiting for.

In a world that rushes intimacy and avoids commitment, Jacob and Rachel stand as a quiet rebuke and a tender hope. They remind us that love does not weaken when it waits—it strengthens. And that sometimes, the years that seem long to everyone else feel like only days to the one who loves truly.

--------------------------------------------------------

## Jacob and Rachel in the Modern world

If Jacob and Rachel were living in the modern world, their relationship would be one that draws attention—not because it is loud, but because it is *enduring*. In a culture that values speed over substance and access over effort, Jacob's willingness to wait and work would feel almost radical. He would not be the man looking for shortcuts or instant gratification. Instead, he would be the one willing to prove love through consistency, sacrifice, and time—qualities often misunderstood as weakness in a world trained to move on quickly.

Jacob would likely be a driven man, shaped by ambition and a complicated family history. He would carry both insecurity and determination, striving to become someone worthy of the promise he believes he carries. In the modern world, this might show up as long hours, multiple responsibilities, or an intense focus on building something lasting. Rachel would be drawn to his devotion, but she would also feel the weight of being deeply loved in a society that constantly measures women by visibility, productivity, and comparison. Her beauty would attract attention, but her deeper struggle would be learning not to let comparison—especially with those closest to her—define her worth.

Their greatest strength in the modern world would be patience—something rarely celebrated, yet desperately needed. They would resist the pressure for premarital intimacy, choosing instead to build emotional and spiritual connection first. In an age where boundaries are often dismissed as outdated, their restraint would require mutual agreement and ongoing discipline. This choice would protect their bond, but it would not shield them from longing. Waiting would test them, forcing honest conversations about desire, timing, and trust.

Their challenges would surface in familiar ways. Rachel might still struggle with comparison and delayed fulfillment, especially if dreams like motherhood, career success, or personal validation take longer than expected. Jacob, focused on provision and perseverance, might unintentionally neglect emotional presence, assuming effort alone communicates love. In a modern marriage, this could create distance—Rachel feeling unseen, Jacob feeling unappreciated. Without intentional communication, patience could turn into quiet resentment.

Yet their love would endure because it is rooted in commitment rather than convenience. Jacob would continue to choose Rachel daily, not just romantically but practically— showing up, providing stability, and refusing to abandon the relationship when it becomes complicated. Rachel, over time, would learn that being chosen consistently is more valuable than being envied publicly. Together, they would grow into a couple whose story reminds others that love worth having is love worth waiting for—and working for.

In a modern world built on immediacy, Jacob and Rachel would quietly testify that perseverance, discipline, and devotion still produce something beautiful.

# 5

# Ruth and Boaz

*Love That Grows from Loyalty, Integrity, and Redemption*

Some love stories arrive like thunder—sudden, loud, unforgettable. The love story of Ruth and Boaz arrives differently. It comes like rain on dry ground, steady and unannounced, soaking into places long forgotten. It is not born of pursuit, but of presence. Not driven by romance, but by righteousness. And because of that, it has become one of the most complete love stories in Scripture—a model not only for marriage, but for how human relationships are meant to honor God, dignity, and destiny.

Ruth enters the biblical story not as a bride, but as a widow. Loss has already marked her life early. She has buried a husband, watched a family unravel, and faced a future stripped of security. Yet what defines Ruth is not what she loses, but what she chooses. When Naomi urges her to return to her own people, Ruth makes a decision that reshapes history. "Where you go, I will go." These are not words of obligation. They are words of covenant. Ruth's loyalty is fierce and uncalculated. She binds herself not only to Naomi, but to Naomi's God, Naomi's grief, and Naomi's uncertain future.

This is the first lesson Ruth and Boaz offer us: love begins with commitment long before romance enters the picture. Ruth does not love to be loved; she loves to be faithful. She chooses presence over comfort, solidarity over self-preservation. In doing so, she steps into a redemptive story she cannot yet see.

Boaz enters the narrative as a man already established— respected, prosperous, and known for his character. He does not come looking for a wife; he comes overseeing his fields with justice. When he notices Ruth, it is not her beauty that captures his attention, but her reputation. He has heard of her loyalty, her sacrifice, her kindness toward Naomi. Boaz recognizes virtue when he sees it, and he responds with protection, not exploitation.

In a time when a foreign woman could easily be mistreated, Boaz draws clear boundaries. He ensures Ruth's safety. He instructs his workers to leave extra grain. He speaks to her with respect, calling her "my daughter," not to diminish her, but to shield her. His integrity is quiet but firm. He does not rush intimacy. He allows trust to grow naturally, rooted in honor.

This is the second great lesson of their love story: attraction must submit to righteousness. Boaz does not confuse opportunity with entitlement. He waits. He watches. He allows God's order to govern his desire.

Ruth, for her part, moves with humility. She does not demand. She does not presume. When Naomi later instructs her to approach Boaz at the threshing floor, Ruth obeys carefully, respectfully, and without manipulation. This moment is often misunderstood, but it is not one of seduction—it is one of surrender. Ruth places herself at Boaz's feet, not to take advantage of him, but to appeal to his role as kinsman-redeemer. She is asking for covering, not conquest.

Boaz's response reveals the depth of his character. He praises her virtue. He reassures her dignity. And then—most importantly—he honors process. Though he has the means and desire to redeem Ruth, he recognizes that another relative has the first legal right. Boaz refuses to bypass justice for personal gain. Love, in his hands, is patient and lawful. He will not build a future on someone else's compromise.

This restraint is the heartbeat of their story. In a world that celebrates shortcuts, Ruth and Boaz show us that love that waits on God is never wasted. Boaz goes to the elders. He settles the matter publicly. He redeems Ruth openly. Their marriage is not secretive or scandalous—it is celebrated and blessed by the community.

The lessons here are profound. Loyalty invites integrity. Integrity creates safety. Safety allows love to flourish. Ruth does not have to chase Boaz; her character speaks for her. Boaz does not have to prove his strength; his righteousness speaks for him. Together, they create a union built not on need, but on mutual honor.

God's redemption is the quiet architect behind it all. Ruth, a Moabite—once excluded—becomes included not by force, but by faithfulness. Boaz, a man of standing, uses his position to restore rather than dominate. Their marriage produces Obed, then Jesse, then David. And from David comes the Messiah. What began as loyalty between two women becomes salvation for nations.

This is why Ruth and Boaz are often held up as the example for all relationships. They show us that love is not merely emotional—it is ethical. It considers others. It honors God's order. It redeems rather than consumes. Their story teaches us that the best relationships are not rushed, not reckless, and not rooted in fear—but in faithfulness.

In the end, Ruth does not just gain a husband. She gains belonging. Boaz does not just gain a wife. He becomes part of a legacy larger than himself. Their love proves that when loyalty and integrity meet, redemption follows.

And perhaps that is the greatest lesson of all: when we choose to love God's way, even the smallest acts of faithfulness can echo through generations.

----------------------------------------------------

## Ruth and Boaz in the Modern World

If Ruth and Boaz were living in the modern world, they would be the couple people point to when they say, "That's how it's supposed to be done." Not because their relationship would be perfect or dramatic, but because it would be marked by clarity, safety, and mutual respect—qualities often missing in modern relationships. Their love would not begin with flirtation or chemistry alone, but with character observed over time, integrity tested in ordinary moments, and trust built without manipulation.

Ruth, in the modern world, would likely be a woman rebuilding her life after loss. She might be a widow, a single mother, or someone starting over in a new city with limited resources. What would distinguish her is not her résumé, but her loyalty. She would be the one who stays when it would be easier to leave, who shows up consistently for family, and who works diligently without entitlement. In a culture that encourages self-preservation above all else, Ruth's commitment to care for Naomi would feel countercultural—choosing relationship over independence, responsibility over escape.

Boaz would be a man known for his reputation long before romance enters the picture. He would be respected in his workplace or community, not because he dominates, but because he protects. He would notice Ruth not through pursuit, but through observation—watching how she treats others, how she works, how she carries herself with humility. In a modern context, Boaz would set boundaries early, refusing to exploit vulnerability or blur lines. He would value transparency, accountability, and doing things "the right way," even when it costs him convenience or time.

Their relationship would unfold slowly. No games. No confusion. Boaz would make his intentions clear without pressure, and Ruth would respond without desperation. In a dating culture plagued by mixed signals and emotional ambiguity, their clarity would feel refreshing. They would involve community—mentors, family, and trusted voices—rather than isolating themselves in secrecy. Their love would be public, honorable, and patient.

The lesson Ruth and Boaz would teach the modern world is simple but powerful: love grows best where dignity is protected. Ruth would not have to compete or perform to be chosen, and Boaz would not have to prove masculinity through conquest. Their bond would be rooted in mutual respect and shared values, allowing romance to emerge naturally rather than forcefully.

In a world hungry for healthy examples, Ruth and Boaz would quietly succeed. Their story would remind us that when loyalty meets integrity, redemption still happens—and love still works, even now.

# 6

# Hannah and Elkanah

*Love That Listens, Love That Prays,*
*Love That Endures*

Some love stories unfold quietly, without spectacle or applause, shaped not by passion but by persistence. The love story of Hannah and Elkanah is one such story. It does not center on dramatic romance or public triumph, but on the sacred work of staying tender in the face of long disappointment. Their relationship reveals what it means to love faithfully when prayers go unanswered, when wounds are private, and when devotion to God must carry what human affection alone cannot heal.

Elkanah loved Hannah deeply. Scripture makes this clear, not through grand gestures, but through consistency. He noticed her pain. He saw her sorrow long before it became public. In a household complicated by polygamy and rivalry, Elkanah's affection for Hannah stood apart. He gave her a double portion—not to shame Peninnah, but to reassure Hannah of her value. His love did not erase her grief, but it refused to dismiss it. This is the first defining feature of their relationship: *love that pays attention*.

Hannah's barrenness was not merely biological; it was social, emotional, and spiritual. In her world, motherhood was identity. Each year that passed without a child was another quiet loss, another unspoken ache. Peninnah's cruelty sharpened that pain, turning private sorrow into public humiliation. And yet, Elkanah did not withdraw. He asked Hannah questions that reveal care, even if they also reveal misunderstanding. "Why is thy heart grieved?" he asked. "Am not I better to thee than ten sons?"

It is here that the complexity of love becomes visible. Elkanah loved Hannah sincerely, but he could not fully enter her pain. His words were meant to comfort, yet they revealed a gap between empathy and experience. This is one of the lessons their story teaches us: love does not require perfect understanding, but it does require presence. Elkanah stayed. He listened. He did not replace Hannah or abandon her. His love was steady, even when his insight was limited.

Hannah, meanwhile, carried her sorrow differently. She did not lash out at Elkanah, nor did she harden herself against God. Instead, she turned inward and upward. Her devotion was quiet but fierce. At Shiloh, she prayed not for spectacle, but for release. Her prayer was wordless, raw, and deeply personal. She poured out her soul before God, refusing to pretend strength she did not feel. This is the second defining feature of their relationship: *faith-centered love that knows where to take its pain*.

Hannah did not blame Elkanah for her barrenness, nor did she demand that he fix what only God could address. She carried her grief without making it his burden to solve. This restraint is not weakness; it is wisdom. Hannah understood that some wounds must be healed by God alone. Her vow—offering her future child back to God—reveals the depth of her faith. She did not see motherhood as possession, but as stewardship.

Elkanah's response to Hannah's vow is subtle but powerful. He does not resist her promise. He does not fear losing what they have waited for so long to receive. Instead, he supports her devotion, saying, "Do what seems best to you." This moment reveals a rare feature in their relationship: *spiritual unity*. Elkanah trusted Hannah's discernment. He honored her spiritual agency. Love, here, does not compete with God—it cooperates with Him.

When Hannah conceives and gives birth to Samuel, joy does not erase sacrifice. True to her vow, Hannah returns Samuel to the Lord. This is not abandonment; it is obedience. Elkanah goes with her. He does not question her resolve or weaken her commitment. Together, they release what they love most. This is perhaps the greatest lesson of their relationship: *love that is willing to give, not just receive*.

Their marriage teaches us that faith-centered love is not transactional. Hannah did not serve God only until her prayer was answered. Elkanah did not support Hannah only when her joy returned. Their devotion endured before, during, and after fulfillment. God honored that faith, blessing Hannah with more children, but the true miracle had already occurred— their love had survived the waiting.

Yet their story is not without its imperfections. Elkanah's polygamy created unnecessary pain, exposing a cultural practice that fractured emotional security. Peninnah's presence intensified Hannah's suffering and reveals the cost of divided affection. This serves as a cautionary lesson: love thrives best where it is undivided and protected. Elkanah's love for Hannah was real, but the structure of his household limited its healing power.

Still, grace moves through the story. Hannah's song of praise becomes prophetic, echoing themes of reversal and redemption that will later resurface in Scripture. Her faith reshapes history. Elkanah's support, quiet and consistent, creates space for her obedience to flourish.

Hannah and Elkanah show us that love is not always loud. Sometimes it looks like sitting beside someone who is hurting and not rushing them toward resolution. Sometimes it looks like praying alone but returning home to someone who still chooses you. Their relationship reminds us that the strongest love stories are not built on ease, but on endurance — on the courage to keep believing together.

In a world that often measures love by outcomes, Hannah and Elkanah teach us to measure it by faithfulness. Love that listens. Love that prays. Love that stays.

--------------------------------------------------------

**Hannah and Elkanah in Modern Times**

If Hannah and Elkanah were living in the modern world, their relationship would be one that outsiders might quietly admire but not fully understand. They would be the couple navigating a deeply personal struggle—infertility—in a society that speaks loudly about options but often listens poorly to pain. Their marriage would not be defined by appearances, but by the quiet work of showing up for one another in seasons that do not resolve quickly.

Elkanah, in the modern world, would be a man who genuinely loves his wife but does not always know how to fix what hurts her. He would be present—attending appointments, remembering dates, noticing shifts in Hannah's mood—but he might still occasionally miss the emotional depth of her grief. His instinct would be reassurance: reminding Hannah of her worth, of their bond, of all that still exists beyond motherhood. At times, his comfort might feel insufficient, even frustrating, not because it lacks love, but because it cannot replace what Hannah longs for. Yet he would remain steady, refusing to withdraw or grow resentful.

Hannah would carry her pain inward, especially in a culture saturated with pregnancy announcements, social media comparisons, and unspoken expectations. She would likely be faithful, private, and prayerful—someone who journals, seeks spiritual counsel, and wrestles honestly with God. Her devotion would not isolate her from Elkanah; instead, it would stabilize the marriage. She would not blame him or allow bitterness to erode respect. Rather, she would learn to hold grief without letting it harden her heart.

Their strength in the modern world would be their shared faith and mutual respect. They would likely seek counseling not as a sign of failure, but as wisdom. Elkanah would learn to listen more deeply, and Hannah would learn that vulnerability is not burdening. Together, they would resist the temptation to let delayed dreams define their identity as a couple.

Hannah and Elkanah would remind the modern world that love does not always remove pain—but it can carry it. Their marriage would be a testimony that faith-centered love, expressed through patience, presence, and prayer, still has the power to endure even the most silent struggles.

# 7

# David and Michal

*Love That Began in Courage and Broke
Under the Weight of Pride and Power*

Some love stories begin in innocence and end in wisdom. Others begin in courage and end in caution. The love story of David and Michal belongs to the latter—a story that shows us not only how love can be real, brave, and selfless, but also how it can be slowly damaged by pride, misalignment, and the intrusion of politics into intimacy. Their relationship offers a blueprint for understanding how love must be protected—not just from enemies outside the home, but from fractures within the heart.

Michal loved David first. Scripture is unambiguous about this, and that alone sets their story apart. In a biblical landscape where women's affections are rarely centered, Michal's love is named, acknowledged, and decisive. She sees David not merely as a warrior or a rising star in her father's court, but as a man worth risking everything for. When Saul's jealousy turns murderous, it is Michal who acts. She lowers David through a window, deceives her father's guards, and places herself squarely in danger to save the man she loves. This is not passive affection. This is courageous love.

Here lies the first foundational truth in their story: love, at its best, is willing to protect. Michal's love is not theoretical; it costs her safety, loyalty to her father, and her standing in the royal household. In this, she models a core blueprint of healthy relationships—*advocacy*. Love does not remain neutral when the beloved is threatened. It chooses sides.

David, for his part, receives Michal's love during a season of survival. He is young, hunted, and learning what it means to be anointed but not yet appointed. Michal's intervention saves his life, but it does not anchor his heart. This is not because David is ungrateful, but because love entered his life during instability. He is running, hiding, becoming. And sometimes, when love meets us in chaos, it struggles to grow roots.

Their marriage, arranged within political tension, is never given the quiet space it needs to mature. Saul uses Michal as leverage, offering her to David not out of paternal generosity, but as a snare. From the beginning, politics invade intimacy. Love is placed under pressure to serve ambition. This is the first major mistake in their relationship: *allowing external power to dictate internal bonds*.

As David flees, Michal is taken from him and given to another man. Her voice is absent in the decision. Her body becomes a bargaining chip in a kingdom obsessed with control. When David later demands her return, it is not framed as romantic longing, but as legal right. This moment reveals a painful truth: love that once saved a life is now reduced to political restitution. David's insistence may be lawful, but it is not tender. He retrieves Michal, but not the intimacy they once shared.

This is the second fracture in their relationship: *when love is not nurtured, it becomes transactional*. David has grown into power. Michal has grown into silence. The courage that once defined her is buried under displacement and disappointment. She returns to a man who has changed—and who no longer sees her the way he once did.

The final break comes not through infidelity or betrayal, but through pride colliding with pain. When David dances before the Lord, unrestrained and unguarded, Michal watches from a window—the same place where she once saved him. This time, however, her heart does not leap with love. It hardens with contempt. She criticizes him, not because she despises God, but because she no longer recognizes the man she married. David's public humility feels, to her, like private dishonor.

Here, both are wrong.

Michal's mistake is rooted in pride shaped by royal upbringing. She measures dignity by appearance, not obedience. She confuses love with image. Her disdain reveals unresolved grief and unspoken resentment—wounds that were never healed because they were never named. David's mistake, on the other hand, is dismissiveness. Instead of hearing the pain beneath her words, he defends himself and distances his heart further. Love, at this point, stops listening.

Their story teaches us a sobering lesson: *love can be genuine and still fail if humility is lost on both sides*. Michal once saved David's life, but pride prevented her from walking with him into spiritual maturity. David once valued Michal's devotion, but power prevented him from tending to her heart.

And yet, their relationship remains foundational—not because it succeeds, but because it warns.

David and Michal show us that love must be protected from role confusion. When one partner outgrows the shared vision and the other clings to status, intimacy erodes. They show us that love cannot survive on history alone. Past sacrifice must be honored continuously, not remembered selectively. They show us that politics—whether royal ambition, career pressure, public image, or family interference—can quietly poison what was once sincere.

Most importantly, they show us that love requires mutual growth. Michal loved David's courage, but struggled to love his calling. David accepted Michal's protection, but did not shepherd her heart when he no longer needed rescue. Love fractured where empathy should have deepened.

Their story is a blueprint not of ideal love, but of *real love*— love that begins with bravery, but demands humility to endure. It reminds us that saving someone is not the same as staying connected to them. That love must evolve as people do. And that without intentional care, even the truest affection can be damaged by silence, pride, and power.

David and Michal loved each other once—truly. And that is why their story matters. It teaches us not just how to love well, but how easily love can be lost when we stop choosing one another in the midst of change.

----------------------------------------------------

## David and Michal in Modern Times

If David and Michal were living in the modern world, their relationship would likely begin with intensity and admiration, the kind that draws people together quickly but tests them just as fast. Michal would be drawn to David's confidence, talent, and calling. In a modern setting, David might be a rising public figure—an artist, activist, athlete, or leader—someone with visible favor and momentum. Michal, raised in privilege or influence, would recognize his potential early and fall in love not only with who he is, but with who he is becoming.

Michal would still be brave. She would be the one who defends David when others turn on him—standing up to family, speaking truth in hostile rooms, risking her reputation to protect him. In the beginning, her loyalty would feel unshakable. David, under pressure and still finding his footing, would lean on her support without fully realizing its cost. Love would form in crisis, and like many modern relationships born under stress, it would bond them quickly but leave little time to build shared rhythms once the storm passes.

As David's life expands—career success, public attention, increasing responsibility—the strain would begin. Power and visibility would change him. Not necessarily for the worse, but enough that the man Michal first loved would feel increasingly distant. David would grow more focused on purpose and public calling, assuming Michal understands without needing reassurance. Michal, meanwhile, would feel unseen, displaced, and privately resentful. Her mistake in the modern world would be silence—allowing disappointment to harden into contempt rather than naming her hurt.

Their final fracture would likely come over image and authenticity. David would embrace freedom, expression, and spiritual passion in ways that feel embarrassing or destabilizing to Michal, who values dignity, order, and control. In a public culture where perception matters, she would criticize what feels like recklessness. David, feeling misunderstood, would respond defensively rather than compassionately. Both would speak past one another—each convinced they are right, neither willing to pause long enough to repair the gap.

In the modern world, David and Michal would show us how love can be real and still fail if it is not tended. They would remind us that admiration must mature into understanding, that support must be reciprocated, and that relationships cannot survive on history alone. Their story would caution modern couples that when pride, public pressure, and unspoken pain go unaddressed, even brave love can quietly break.

# 8

# Hosea and Gomer

*Love That Hurts, Love That Holds, Love That Refuses to Let Go*

The love story of Hosea and Gomer is not a romance anyone would choose, yet it is one no one forgets. It is raw and unsettling, stripped of sentimentality and comfort. Where other biblical love stories inspire hope through harmony, this one teaches through heartbreak. Hosea and Gomer reveal the anatomy of covenant love—the kind of love that does not retreat when betrayed, the kind that stays when pride begs it to leave. It is a love that mirrors God's heart more closely than any other, precisely because it costs so much.

Hosea enters the story as a faithful man called to live out a faithful message. His marriage is not accidental; it is commanded. God instructs him to marry Gomer, a woman whose unfaithfulness will not be hypothetical but habitual. From the beginning, Hosea's love is marked by obedience rather than desire. This alone reframes the meaning of love. Love, here, is not rooted in compatibility or romance—it is rooted in covenant and calling.

Gomer, by contrast, is restless. She is drawn to affection that demands nothing and offers little. She does not reject Hosea because he is cruel or absent; she rejects him because faithfulness feels restrictive to a wounded heart. Her unfaithfulness is not merely sexual—it is emotional, spiritual, and relational. She seeks validation elsewhere, mistaking attention for worth. This is the first lesson their relationship teaches us: betrayal often grows from unresolved emptiness, not outright malice.

Hosea's pain is quiet but consuming. Each time Gomer leaves, he feels the humiliation not only of a betrayed husband, but of a public figure whose private life has become a living sermon. Yet Hosea does not respond with rage. He does not shame her publicly. He names the truth, mourns the loss, and waits. This is covenant love in its most difficult form—love that holds boundaries while still holding hope.

Gomer's mistake is clear: she confuses freedom with abandonment. She believes that independence will satisfy her, but it leaves her increasingly vulnerable. Over time, her lovers fail her. The gifts stop. The protection disappears. She is reduced from desired to discarded. And here, Scripture offers one of its most devastating images—Gomer sold, stripped of dignity, standing in the marketplace of her own poor decisions.

Hosea's response is not vengeance. It is redemption.

He goes to her. He pays for her. He brings her home.

This moment is the emotional core of their story. Hosea does not rescue Gomer because she has proven herself changed; he rescues her because covenant does not wait for worthiness. This is the second great lesson: true love does not erase consequences, but it offers restoration beyond them. Hosea does not pretend the betrayal never happened. He requires healing, separation, and rebuilding. Love, here, is not permissive—it is redemptive.

Yet Hosea's mistake is also worth naming. In bearing the weight of divine symbolism, he risks losing himself. Faithfulness without boundaries can become self-erasure if it is not guided by God. Hosea's strength is his obedience, but his vulnerability is emotional exhaustion. Covenant love must be sustained by God, or it collapses under its own sacrifice.

The story quietly warns us that loving the broken requires divine support—not human endurance alone.

What makes this love story foundational is not its pain, but its clarity. Hosea and Gomer reveal that love is not defined by how it begins, but by how it responds to betrayal. They show us that covenant is not a contract that dissolves at first offense, nor is it blind tolerance of harm. It is a commitment to truth, correction, and restoration when possible.

Their relationship teaches us several enduring lessons:

First, love cannot heal what it refuses to confront. Hosea names Gomer's unfaithfulness plainly. He does not soften reality to preserve comfort. Love that heals must be honest.

Second, betrayal does not cancel dignity. Even at her lowest point, Gomer is still pursued. Still named. Still valued. Love restores identity before it restores relationship.

Third, redemption is costly. Hosea pays—not only with money, but with reputation, patience, and pain. Love that mirrors God's love always costs the one who gives it most.

Finally, Hosea and Gomer teach us that love is strongest when rooted in purpose beyond emotion. Hosea's love survives because it is anchored in obedience to God. Without that anchor, such faithfulness would be impossible.

This story mirrors God's relationship with Israel, but it also mirrors our relationships with one another. We are all, at times, Hosea—loving beyond what feels fair. And at times, we are Gomer—seeking fulfillment in places that cannot keep us. The story does not glorify betrayal, nor does it trivialize pain. It dignifies both by showing that redemption is real, but never cheap.

Hosea and Gomer's love story is painful because it tells the truth. It is powerful because it refuses to end in abandonment. It stands as a reminder that covenant love is not about perfection—it is about persistence, truth, and the willingness to choose redemption again and again.

And in that choosing, we glimpse the heart of God Himself.

------------------------------------------------------

**Hosea and Gomer in Modern Times**

If Hosea and Gomer were living in the modern world, their relationship would be one of the most uncomfortable—and most debated—stories people encounter. It would not fit neatly into modern categories of empowerment or self-care, yet it would force hard conversations about covenant, accountability, and redemption. Many would question Hosea's decision to stay. Others would judge Gomer harshly. And yet, their story would expose the tension between love that endures and love that protects itself.

Hosea, in the modern world, would likely be a man of deep conviction—perhaps a pastor, counselor, or community leader—whose private life becomes inseparable from his public calling. His willingness to remain faithful would be misunderstood as weakness by some and praised as virtue by others. The greatest challenge he would face is discernment: knowing when love means pursuing and when love means setting boundaries. In a culture that often equates forgiveness with enabling, Hosea would have to rely heavily on God to ensure his compassion does not become self-destruction.

Gomer, by contrast, would struggle loudly in a world saturated with validation and escape routes. Social media, casual relationships, and endless options would amplify her search for worth. Her unfaithfulness would not simply be physical, but emotional—seeking affirmation wherever it is easiest to find. In the modern world, her story would likely be labeled as trauma, insecurity, or addiction. And while those explanations might offer insight, they would not remove responsibility. Gomer's greatest battle would be learning that attention is not love and that freedom without commitment often leads to deeper captivity.

If redemption were to occur, it would require structure. Therapy, accountability, separation, and rebuilding trust would be essential. Hosea's love would need boundaries to remain healthy, and Gomer's return would require genuine repentance, not just regret. Their relationship could survive— but only if love is anchored in truth rather than emotion alone.

In the modern world, Hosea and Gomer would remind us that not every broken relationship should be restored, but some— by God's design—are meant to reveal the depth of covenant love. Their story would challenge modern culture to reconsider whether love is merely about self-fulfillment, or about transformation.

# 9

# Esther and King Ahasuerus

*Love, Power, and the Courage That Turned Favor into Salvation*

Some love stories are born in tenderness. Others are born in survival. The story of Esther and King Ahasuerus unfolds in the uneasy space where affection meets authority, where vulnerability stands in the shadow of power, and where love— if it can be called that—must mature into responsibility before it can become redemptive. Their relationship is complex, imperfect, and deeply instructive, offering lessons not about ideal romance, but about courage, wisdom, and the quiet ways God uses flawed human systems to protect His people.

Esther enters the story not as a woman seeking influence, but as a young woman swept into it. She is chosen not by pursuit, but by circumstance. Her beauty places her in the king's sight, but it is her spirit—unassuming, observant, disciplined—that allows her to remain there. Esther does not arrive demanding power. She learns first how to listen. She watches the court. She heeds Mordecai's counsel. In a world ruled by impulse and excess, Esther survives by restraint.

King Ahasuerus, by contrast, is a man accustomed to absolute authority. His early decisions reveal volatility—banishing Vashti in wounded pride, surrounding himself with advisors who reflect his own insecurity, allowing policies to be shaped by emotion rather than wisdom. This is the first mistake in the relationship: *power exercised without discernment*. Ahasuerus does not yet know how to separate ego from leadership, or desire from responsibility.

Esther's position as queen does not immediately alter this dynamic. She holds favor, but favor alone is fragile. The king's affection for her is real, yet shallow at first—rooted more in delight than understanding. Esther is loved, but not yet known. And this is where the second lesson begins to form: *favor without wisdom cannot sustain protection*. Love that does not grow in understanding remains vulnerable to manipulation.

Haman's rise exposes this vulnerability. The king, still governing reactively, entrusts power too freely. He signs a decree of destruction without asking who will be harmed. This is Ahasuerus's second great mistake—not cruelty, but carelessness. He does not hate the Israelites; he simply fails to see them. And unseen people are easily endangered.

Esther, now fully aware of the cost of silence, faces her defining moment. Her relationship with the king has brought her access, but access alone does not guarantee safety. To speak is to risk rejection. To remain silent is to allow destruction. Esther's courage does not erupt dramatically—it gathers slowly, shaped by prayer, fasting, and communal support. This is where the relationship transforms.

Esther approaches the king not as a frightened girl or a demanding queen, but as a wise woman who understands timing. She does not accuse. She invites. She does not overwhelm him with truth before his heart is ready to receive it. Her wisdom lies in patience. She creates space for the king to listen, to reflect, to awaken to the weight of his own authority.

Here we see the most important lesson of their relationship: *true influence does not force power—it guides it*. Esther does not dominate Ahasuerus; she educates him. She does not manipulate; she reveals. Her courage is quiet but firm, rooted not in emotion, but in responsibility to a people she has not yet publicly claimed.

When Esther finally reveals her identity and the threat against her people, the king is confronted with the consequences of his negligence. His anger burns—but this time, not in pride. This time, it is righteous. Ahasuerus begins to change. He listens. He acts. He corrects. Love—now tempered by accountability—becomes protective.

Yet the relationship is not without its flaws even in deliverance. The king cannot revoke the original decree, bound by the rigidity of his own laws. Instead, he offers Esther and Mordecai authority to counter it. This highlights another lesson: *even well-intentioned power is limited when systems are unjust*. Redemption often requires creativity when mistakes cannot be undone.

Esther's courage saves her people, but it also reshapes her relationship with the king. She is no longer merely favored— she is trusted. No longer ornamental—she is influential. Their relationship matures from attraction into partnership, from surface affection into shared responsibility. This is the redemptive arc of their story.

Yet we must be honest about the mistakes. Ahasuerus's impulsiveness created the danger in the first place. Esther's initial silence, though understandable, delayed intervention. Their story reminds us that love and leadership both require vigilance. Silence can be strategic, but it must not become fear. Authority can be powerful, but it must be accountable.

The love story of Esther and Ahasuerus is not foundational because it models romance—it is foundational because it models *transformation*. It shows how courage can redeem flawed power, how wisdom can steady volatile affection, and how God can use imperfect relationships to accomplish perfect deliverance.

Esther's bravery turns favor into salvation. Ahasuerus's willingness to listen turns authority into protection. Together, they stand as a reminder that love—when joined with courage and humility—can become a vessel for justice.

Their story teaches us that relationships do not have to begin well to end redemptively. That influence is most powerful when exercised with wisdom. And that sometimes, love's greatest achievement is not intimacy, but the protection of others.

In the end, Esther and King Ahasuerus reveal a truth as relevant now as it was then: when courage meets responsibility, and favor submits to wisdom, love—however imperfect—can change the course of history.

-------------------------------------------------------------

## Esther and King Ahasuerus in Modern Times

If Esther and King Ahasuerus were living in the modern world, their relationship would unfold within systems of power, influence, and public scrutiny rather than royal courts and decrees. Ahasuerus would likely be a high-level executive, political leader, or public figure accustomed to authority and surrounded by advisors who affirm his decisions more than they challenge them. Esther might enter his life through visibility—education, media, or professional excellence—but she would not initially seek influence. Her strength would be her restraint, her discernment, and her ability to read rooms before she speaks.

In a modern context, Esther's greatest challenge would be learning when silence protects and when it endangers. Early in the relationship, she might downplay her identity, values, or convictions in order to survive within a powerful system not designed with her in mind. Ahasuerus's mistake would mirror his ancient one: making decisions too quickly, trusting the wrong voices, and failing to recognize how his power affects those with less protection. Love, at first, would be real but shallow—rooted in admiration rather than understanding.

The turning point would come when Esther recognizes that access without courage changes nothing. In the modern world, this might look like whistleblowing, advocacy, or using her platform to protect marginalized people at personal risk. Her wisdom would be evident in how she approaches Ahasuerus—not confrontational, not manipulative, but strategic and grounded in truth. She would understand that influence is most effective when paired with timing and clarity.

If growth occurs, Ahasuerus would learn to listen. Exposure to Esther's courage would confront his complacency, forcing him to reckon with the consequences of unchecked authority. Their relationship would mature from surface affection into mutual respect, with Esther no longer merely admired, but trusted. Mistakes would still exist—systems would still be flawed—but redemption would come through accountability.

In the modern world, Esther and Ahasuerus would show that relationships shaped by power can either enable harm or become instruments of protection. Their story would remind us that courage transforms favor into responsibility, and that love—when paired with wisdom—can still change outcomes far beyond itself.

# 10

# Joseph and Asenath

*Love After Loss, and the Quiet Work of Restoration*

Some love stories are born in innocence. Others are born in recovery. The love story of Joseph and Asenath emerges not from youthful longing or dramatic pursuit, but from survival— after betrayal, after imprisonment, after the long work of learning how to trust again. Their union is not loud or romanticized in Scripture, yet it carries one of the most powerful messages of all: love does not have to begin early to be real, and trauma does not disqualify the heart from joy.

Joseph arrives at marriage not as a dreamer, but as a man who has endured. His life has been shaped by rejection—sold by his brothers, stripped of status, falsely accused, forgotten in prison. Betrayal taught him caution. Injustice taught him restraint. Yet what is remarkable about Joseph is not that he survives suffering, but that he does not allow suffering to poison his character. When God elevates him to power in Egypt, Joseph carries authority without bitterness and wisdom without cruelty. This emotional maturity becomes the soil in which love can finally grow.

Asenath enters Joseph's life not during his vulnerability, but during his restoration. She is given to him after he has been publicly vindicated, after his gifts are recognized, after his identity is secure. This timing matters. Joseph does not marry while wounded and reactive. He marries after healing has begun. The first lesson of their relationship is clear: *restored love requires restored identity*. Joseph is no longer trying to prove himself. He is ready to share his life rather than seek validation from another.

Asenath herself represents transformation. She is not merely a political match; she is a woman stepping into a new way of life. Though Scripture is brief about her inner journey, tradition paints her as one who turns from idols toward the God Joseph serves. This matters deeply. Their relationship is not built on infatuation, but on alignment. Asenath does not ask Joseph to shrink his faith to fit her world. She expands her world to meet his values. This is the second lesson: *love grows strongest when values converge, not compete*.

Their marriage is marked by stability rather than drama. Joseph, once stripped of control, now governs with order. Asenath, once surrounded by excess, now lives within purpose. Together, they create a home shaped by gratitude rather than entitlement. Their sons' names reveal Joseph's healing: Manasseh—"God has made me forget all my hardship"—and Ephraim—"God has made me fruitful in the land of my affliction." These names are not denial; they are testimony. Joseph does not erase the past—he redeems it.

Yet even this love story is not without its quiet challenges. Joseph's mistake lies not in wrongdoing, but in emotional distance. Trauma teaches self-reliance, and Joseph has learned to carry burdens alone. While he is faithful and present, there is a guardedness about him. Power can become a shield. Responsibility can replace vulnerability. This is a subtle but real challenge in relationships formed after trauma: the instinct to protect oneself even when safety has returned.

Asenath's potential mistake mirrors this in a different way. Coming from privilege and abundance, she must learn patience with Joseph's depth. His silence is not indifference; it is reflection. His caution is not mistrust; it is memory. Love between them requires understanding that healing is ongoing. Restoration is not a moment—it is a process.

Their relationship teaches us that love after trauma must be gentle. Joseph does not rush intimacy. Asenath does not demand access to wounds she did not witness. Their bond grows through shared purpose, not forced disclosure. This is perhaps the most important lesson of their love: *not all love stories need to explain the past to honor the future*.

God's role in their union is unmistakable. Joseph does not seek a wife as compensation for suffering. Love is not presented as reward, but as continuation. God restores Joseph's capacity to love without asking him to forget what shaped him. Asenath becomes part of Joseph's redemption story—not as a savior, but as a companion.

In their marriage, we see that God restores more than position. He restores intimacy. He restores the ability to trust, to build, to hope again. Joseph's life teaches us that betrayal does not have to make us bitter, and imprisonment does not have to make us closed. When healing is allowed to take root, love can arrive without fear.

Joseph and Asenath stand as a quiet testament to second beginnings. Their love does not shout, but it stands firm. It is proof that God can bring beauty after devastation, and partnership after isolation. It reminds us that the heart—once broken, but surrendered—can love again, not recklessly, but wisely.

Their story tells us this: restoration does not mean returning to who you were before the pain. It means becoming someone who can love *because* of what you survived, not in spite of it.

-------------------------------------------------------------

**Joseph and Asenath in the Modern World**

If Joseph and Asenath were living in the modern world, their relationship would likely be described as calm, grounded, and quietly resilient. They would not be the couple broadcasting their story on social media or seeking validation from public opinion. Their strength would lie in stability—earned, not assumed. Joseph would enter the relationship as someone who has survived deep betrayal and institutional injustice. In a modern context, this might look like family estrangement, wrongful incarceration, or professional sabotage. These experiences would shape him into a man of discipline, discernment, and emotional restraint.

Joseph's greatest challenge in the modern world would be learning that safety does not require constant vigilance. Trauma teaches people to be self-sufficient, to stay guarded, and to trust slowly. In a relationship, this could show up as emotional reserve—being present and responsible, but hesitant to fully open the deepest layers of pain. Joseph would provide consistency, integrity, and leadership, yet still need space to learn that vulnerability is not weakness when trust has been earned.

Asenath, in the modern world, would likely come from a position of comfort or influence—perhaps raised in privilege, status, or cultural advantage. Her transition into Joseph's life would require humility and adaptability. She would need to understand that Joseph's silence is not distance, but processing. Her mistake, at times, might be impatience—wanting emotional access faster than healing allows. But her willingness to align with Joseph's values would be the cornerstone of their success.

Together, they would form a partnership built on shared purpose rather than emotional intensity. Their home would be structured, intentional, and forward-looking. They would likely excel in building something meaningful—family, community work, or leadership roles—because both understand responsibility. In a world that often rushes intimacy without healing, Joseph and Asenath would model a relationship where restoration comes first, and love grows safely within it.

Their story in the modern world would remind others that past trauma does not disqualify anyone from healthy love—and that when healing and alignment come together, stability itself can be a form of romance.

# 11

# Samson and Delilah

*When Desire Replaces Discernment*

Some love stories warn us not by how they begin, but by how they unravel. The story of Samson and Delilah is not a romance shaped by patience or covenant; it is a collision of strength and seduction, purpose and appetite. It teaches us that love without discernment can become self-destruction, and that intimacy offered to the wrong person can dismantle even the strongest calling. Their relationship is not the blueprint of healthy love—but it is a foundational lesson in what happens when desire outruns wisdom.

Samson enters the story already marked by destiny. Set apart from birth, consecrated with vows he did not choose but was born into, he carries supernatural strength that reflects divine purpose. Yet Samson's greatest struggle is not his enemies—it is his appetite. Again and again, he is drawn to what looks good rather than what is good for him. His relationships reflect this pattern. He desires quickly, chooses impulsively, and confuses attraction with alignment.

Delilah appears in his life not as a stranger, but as a test Samson should have recognized. She is observant, persistent, and financially motivated by those who oppose him. But Scripture does not present Delilah as a sorceress or villain in disguise. She is a woman who knows what she wants and how to get it. The tragedy is not that Delilah deceives Samson—the tragedy is that Samson keeps telling her the truth while knowing she cannot be trusted.

This is the first and most painful lesson of their relationship: *love requires discernment, not just affection*. Samson confuses emotional intimacy with safety. He mistakes proximity for loyalty. He assumes that strength exempts him from consequence. And in doing so, he places sacred information into careless hands.

Delilah's mistake is equally profound, though of a different kind. She prioritizes profit over people. Whatever tenderness may exist between them is overridden by her willingness to trade Samson's vulnerability for silver. Her persistence is not rooted in love, but in advantage. Each time she presses Samson for the source of his strength, she reveals her agenda. She does not protect what is sacred to him; she exploits it.

Samson's fatal error is not that he loves Delilah — it is that he *reveals himself without requiring trustworthiness*. He toys with the truth until the truth costs him everything. When he finally discloses the source of his strength, it is not because Delilah has proven faithful, but because he is emotionally worn down. Love, when unguarded, becomes manipulation's easiest entry point.

The loss that follows is devastating. Samson's hair is cut. His strength leaves him. His eyes are gouged out. The man who once moved freely is bound, humiliated, and put on display. This is the consequence of misplaced intimacy. The story does not suggest that Delilah physically overpowered Samson—she simply outlasted his boundaries. This reveals another critical lesson: *strength without self-control is not strength at all*.

Yet even in this collapse, the story does not end in despair. Samson's suffering becomes a place of reflection. Blind and imprisoned, he begins to understand what he lost—not just his strength, but his alignment with God. His final prayer is not for restoration of pleasure, but of purpose. And God answers.

Samson's last act accomplishes what his undisciplined life often undermined: deliverance for his people.

The relationship between Samson and Delilah teaches us that love must be stewarded carefully. Not everyone who desires you is safe. Not everyone who touches your life deserves access to your calling. Samson's mistake was assuming that passion could coexist with disobedience without consequence. Delilah's mistake was believing that personal gain would outweigh moral responsibility.

Their story warns us against romanticizing intensity while ignoring integrity. It shows us how easily calling can be compromised when boundaries are blurred. And it reminds us that betrayal often enters through familiarity, not force.

In the end, Samson and Delilah stand as a cautionary tale — not because love is dangerous, but because love without wisdom is. Their story urges us to ask hard questions: Who has access to our vulnerabilities? Who benefits from our weakness? Who protects what is sacred to us?

This is not a story about the failure of love — it is a story about the cost of ignoring truth. And in that cost, it offers a sobering, necessary lesson: desire can blind, but discernment can save.

-------------------------------------------------------------

## Sampson and Delilah in the Modern World

If Samson and Delilah were living in the modern world, their relationship would likely be intense, volatile, and widely misunderstood. It would begin with undeniable chemistry—an attraction that feels electric and consuming. Samson would be a man gifted, talented, and visibly strong in his field—perhaps an athlete, influencer, or public figure—someone accustomed to admiration and confident in his own resilience. Delilah would be perceptive, charming, and strategic, able to read Samson's desires and insecurities with unsettling accuracy.

In a modern setting, Samson's greatest struggle would be boundaries. He would assume that strength, success, or spiritual gifting makes him untouchable. He would overshare with Delilah, mistaking emotional closeness for safety, revealing vulnerabilities that should have been protected. Delilah, meanwhile, would be motivated less by love and more by leverage—information, access, or advantage. Her mistake would be prioritizing gain over care, treating intimacy as a transaction rather than a trust.

Their relationship would likely play out in cycles—passion followed by tension, reconciliation followed by repeated warning signs ignored. Friends and mentors might caution Samson, but he would dismiss concern as jealousy or fear. Delilah would press boundaries subtly, asking questions that seem harmless until they are not. In the modern world, this could look like exploiting secrets, undermining values, or encouraging choices that slowly erode Samson's discipline.

The collapse would be public. Samson's downfall would not come from sudden attack, but from gradual compromise. Career loss, public scandal, or moral failure would follow, leaving him stripped of influence and isolated. Only in the aftermath would clarity arrive. Like the biblical account, his restoration would begin in humility—recognizing that strength without self-control is fragile.

In the modern world, Samson and Delilah would serve as a cautionary mirror. Their relationship would remind us that attraction without discernment leads to destruction, and that not everyone who draws close is meant to be trusted with what makes us strong.

# 12

# King Ahab and Jezebel

*When Love Enables the Wrong Voice*

Some love stories teach us how to build. Others teach us what to guard against. The love story of King Ahab and Jezebel belongs to the latter—not because love was absent, but because it was misdirected. Their relationship reveals how intimacy, when joined to insecurity and unchecked influence, can corrode conscience and distort calling. Ahab and Jezebel show us that love, when it silences truth and empowers manipulation, can become destructive not only to a marriage, but to an entire nation.

Ahab enters the story as a king with authority but little resolve. He inherits power, not purpose. Though positioned to lead Israel with justice, he lacks the inner strength to govern his own desires. Ahab is not cruel by nature; he is weak by inclination. His defining flaw is passivity—an unwillingness to confront, decide, or resist when pressure mounts. This is the soil in which Jezebel's influence takes root.

Jezebel, by contrast, is decisive, commanding, and unapologetically driven. She knows who she is and what she wants. She enters Ahab's life not merely as a wife, but as a force. Raised in a culture that worships power through Baal and control through intimidation, Jezebel does not adapt to Israel's covenant—she seeks to replace it. Her love is not nurturing; it is possessive. She does not strengthen Ahab's leadership; she supplants it.

Their relationship is marked by imbalance from the start. Ahab loves Jezebel, but he also fears her. He yields space where he should have set boundaries. Jezebel mistakes this submission for loyalty and uses it to advance her own agenda. This is the first great lesson of their love story: *love without shared values will eventually demand surrender from one side*. Ahab surrenders his spiritual responsibility. Jezebel never relinquishes control.

The story of Naboth's vineyard exposes the heart of their relationship. Ahab desires what does not belong to him and responds like a child denied a toy—sullen, withdrawn, resentful. Jezebel steps in, not to correct him, but to enable him. She mocks his weakness, then orchestrates murder to satisfy his appetite. Ahab does not plan the crime, but he accepts its fruit. This is the most damning mistake they make together: *one partner commits evil, the other consents through silence.*

Their marriage teaches us that wrongdoing does not require equal participation—only shared benefit. Jezebel's hands are bloody, but Ahab's heart is complicit. Love becomes the justification for injustice. Loyalty replaces morality. And in doing so, their relationship abandons any claim to righteousness.

Jezebel's mistake is rooted in arrogance. She believes power grants immunity. She silences prophets, persecutes truth, and mocks accountability. Her confidence is not faith—it is defiance. She does not fear consequence because she has never been corrected. Love, for her, is dominance. Partnership is conquest.

Ahab's mistake is more tragic because it is quieter. He knows better. He hears Elijah's warnings. He recognizes truth when confronted with it. Yet he lacks the courage to separate himself from Jezebel's influence. His love becomes an excuse for disobedience. He chooses peace in his household over obedience to God. And in doing so, he loses both.

Their relationship offers painful lessons.

First, love that does not honor God will eventually war against truth. Jezebel does not merely practice idolatry; she institutionalizes it. Ahab allows it. What begins as marital compromise becomes national collapse.

Second, strength without humility becomes tyranny, and gentleness without courage becomes weakness. Jezebel's dominance and Ahab's passivity feed each other in a destructive cycle. Neither grows. Neither yields. Neither repents together.

Third, silence is not neutrality. Ahab's failure to confront Jezebel makes him responsible for what he allows. Love does not excuse abdication. Partnership does not eliminate accountability.

And yet, even here, grace flickers. Ahab humbles himself briefly when judgment is pronounced. God delays disaster, revealing that repentance—even late—is still noticed. But Jezebel never bends. Her end is fitting and final, not because God is cruel, but because she refuses correction entirely.

The love story of Ahab and Jezebel is not remembered because it is passionate, but because it is instructive. It shows us that relationships magnify character—for better or worse.

When one partner refuses accountability and the other refuses responsibility, love becomes dangerous.

Ahab and Jezebel remind us that who we love influences who we become. That partnership is never neutral. And that love, when divorced from truth, does not save—it destroys.

Their story stands as a warning written in the language of intimacy: choose wisely who has your ear, your loyalty, and your silence. Because love does not merely affect the heart— it shapes destiny.

-------------------------------------------------------------

## King Ahab and Jezebel in the Modern World

If King Ahab and Jezebel were living in the modern world, their relationship would likely unfold in the public eye—highly visible, highly influential, and deeply polarizing. Ahab would be a man in a position of power—perhaps a politician, corporate leader, or public official—who holds authority on paper but struggles with confidence and conviction. Jezebel would be his strongest voice, his most trusted advisor, and the force behind many of his decisions. To outsiders, she would appear capable, commanding, and fiercely loyal. To those paying closer attention, she would be controlling.

In a modern setting, Ahab's greatest weakness would be avoidance. Rather than confronting conflict, he would defer— to his spouse, to advisors, to whoever speaks most forcefully.

Jezebel would fill that vacuum easily. She would manage narratives, silence opposition, and justify questionable decisions in the name of loyalty or progress. Her mistake would be believing that power and influence excuse ethical compromise. She would see rules as obstacles, not safeguards.

Their relationship would thrive on mutual benefit but lack moral balance. Jezebel would protect Ahab from discomfort; Ahab would protect Jezebel from accountability. Together, they would enable one another's worst instincts. In the modern world, this might look like corruption, silencing whistleblowers, exploiting systems, or weaponizing influence against critics. Love would be used as justification: *I did it for us.*

What their story would reveal today is how dangerous it is when affection replaces integrity. Ahab and Jezebel would remind modern couples that love must never override conscience, and that partnership without shared values eventually becomes destructive. Their relationship would stand as a warning that unchecked influence—especially within intimacy—can quietly erode both character and community.

# 13

# Mary and Joseph

*Love That Chose Obedience Over*
*Understanding*

Some love stories are loud with passion and promise. Others are quiet, forged in uncertainty and sustained by faith. The love story of Mary and Joseph belongs to the second kind. It is not built on ease or explanation, but on obedience—on two people choosing trust in God when circumstances offer little reassurance. Their relationship teaches us that love does not always begin with clarity, but it must always decide whether it will walk in truth.

Mary enters the story as a young woman with a simple life and a steady faith. She is not seeking attention, influence, or distinction when the angel appears. She is chosen, not because she is ambitious, but because she is willing. Her response—"Be it unto me according to thy word"—reveals a heart trained in surrender. Yet acceptance does not erase fear. Mary's calling immediately places her at risk—socially, emotionally, and relationally. Obedience, in her case, costs reputation before it brings purpose.

Joseph's introduction is quieter, but no less significant. He is described as just—a man guided by righteousness rather than impulse. When Mary's pregnancy becomes evident, Joseph faces a crisis that strikes at the core of trust. He has not yet heard from God. All he sees is evidence that contradicts everything he believes about Mary and about their future. His initial decision to put her away privately is not cruelty; it is restraint. This is the first lesson of their relationship: *love does not rush to expose or punish*. Even in confusion, Joseph seeks to protect Mary's dignity.

Yet this moment also reveals their first mistake—not sin, but limitation. Joseph acts before understanding. Mary, though obedient to God, carries her burden silently, unable to explain what cannot yet be believed. Their relationship enters a season where truth exists, but clarity does not. This is the tension many relationships face: when obedience to God outpaces mutual understanding.

God intervenes, not with rebuke, but with reassurance. The angel speaks to Joseph, naming his fear and answering it. Joseph is asked to trust not only God, but Mary. And he does. This choice defines the rest of his life. Joseph takes Mary as his wife, fully aware that whispers will follow, that assumptions will linger, and that his role will be questioned. Love, here, becomes an act of courage.

Joseph protects Mary's honor not with words, but with presence. He stays. He claims responsibility. He shelters her during travel, during birth, during danger. He raises a child not biologically his own without bitterness or distance. This is the second great lesson of their love: *true love is willing to bear weight it did not create*. Joseph does not compete with God's purpose; he cooperates with it.

Mary, for her part, does not diminish Joseph's role. Though chosen uniquely by God, she remains humble. She treasures moments quietly. She submits to partnership rather than elevating her experience above their union. Her mistake—subtle and human—comes later, when she and Joseph assume Jesus is safely among family during travel. Losing Him temporarily reveals a shared oversight: even faithful parents can become complacent. Love and devotion do not exempt us from vigilance.

Yet when Jesus is found, Mary does not lash out in anger; she speaks from concern. Joseph does not assert authority; he listens. Their response models accountability rather than defensiveness. This is another lesson their relationship offers: *mistakes do not destroy love when humility follows*.

Their marriage unfolds largely in silence. Scripture does not record grand declarations of affection, but it reveals consistent faithfulness. Joseph listens when God speaks—whether in dreams warning him to flee, to return, or to wait. Mary follows, trusting the man who trusted her when the world could have turned away. Their love is shaped not by romance, but by shared obedience.

Together, they navigate exile, poverty, misunderstanding, and danger. Their relationship matures under pressure. Joseph never seeks recognition for raising the Son of God. Mary never claims privilege because of her calling. Love, in their hands, remains grounded.

The greatest lesson of Mary and Joseph's love story is this: *love rooted in obedience outlasts confusion*. Trust does not require full understanding, only willingness. Joseph's faithfulness gives Jesus a covering of stability. Mary's devotion gives Him nurture and truth. Neither role overshadows the other. Their partnership reveals that love does not need to be dramatic to be transformative.

Mary and Joseph remind us that the strongest relationships are often the quietest—built not on certainty, but on courage. Their love teaches us that honor can be protected, responsibility can be shared, and faith can hold two people together when explanation fails.

In a world that demands answers before commitment, their story whispers a deeper truth: love sometimes must choose obedience first—and understanding will follow in time.

---------------------------------------------------------

## Joseph and Mary in the Modern World

If Mary and Joseph were living in the modern world, their relationship would almost certainly be pulled into the glare of public opinion. It would not begin as a love story the world celebrates, but as a controversy the world scrutinizes. Yes— there would be tabloids, comment sections, and endless speculation. A young woman pregnant before marriage. A man who stays. A story no one fully believes. In today's culture of instant judgment and viral narratives, Mary and Joseph would be talked about long before they are understood.

Mary would become a subject of suspicion and debate. Social media would dissect her character, question her credibility, and assign motives she never claimed. Some would call her brave. Others would call her reckless. Very few would pause to consider her obedience or the cost of her silence. Mary would not respond with public explanations or online defenses. Her strength would still be quiet. She would protect what is sacred rather than perform transparency for validation. In a world that demands constant disclosure, her restraint would feel unsettling—and powerful.

Joseph would be equally scrutinized. Headlines would question his masculinity, his judgment, his self-respect. Staying would be framed as foolishness by some and heroism by others. He would be accused of being manipulated or naïve. Yet Joseph would choose privacy over publicity. He would not argue with strangers or attempt to control the narrative. His love would be proven not through statements, but through consistency—showing up, providing stability, and refusing to abandon Mary under pressure.

Their relationship would likely withdraw from the noise. They would limit access, protect boundaries, and rely on trusted community rather than public approval. While others monetize their story, Mary and Joseph would live it. They would understand that not every truth is meant for mass consumption, and not every relationship is strengthened by visibility.

In the modern world, Mary and Joseph would remind us that love grounded in obedience does not need an audience. Their relationship would teach that faithfulness often looks foolish to outsiders, and that the most sacred stories are rarely meant to trend.

# 14

# Zechariah and Elizabeth

*Love That Waited in Righteousness and Spoke in God's Time*

Some love stories announce themselves with urgency. Others unfold slowly, shaped by years of faithfulness that rarely draw attention. The love story of Zechariah and Elizabeth belongs to the latter. It is a story of devotion that outlasts disappointment, of righteousness practiced without reward, and of love that remains tender even when prayers seem unanswered. Their marriage teaches us that some of the most anointed outcomes are born not from urgency, but from endurance.

Zechariah and Elizabeth are introduced not through drama, but through description: *they were both righteous before God, walking blamelessly in all the commandments and ordinances of the Lord*. This single sentence tells us more about their relationship than grand gestures ever could. They shared values. They shared faith. They shared a way of life shaped by obedience rather than convenience. Their love was not performative—it was practiced daily, quietly, faithfully.

Yet righteousness did not shield them from pain. Elizabeth was barren, and both were advanced in years. In a culture where fruitfulness was equated with favor, this absence would have been heavy. Their neighbors likely whispered. Their prayers likely grew tired. And yet, Scripture never suggests bitterness between them. This is the first defining feature of their relationship: *shared disappointment did not become shared resentment*. They did not turn on each other. They turned toward God.

Zechariah served as a priest, faithful in his duties even when his personal life felt unresolved. Elizabeth carried her grief privately, bearing not only childlessness, but the social weight of it. Still, she remained devoted—to God and to her husband. Their marriage did not fracture under delayed fulfillment.

Instead, it matured. Love, for them, became a place of refuge rather than accusation.

When the angel appears to Zechariah in the temple, the moment is both sacred and unsettling. God speaks promise into a place long resigned to silence. Yet Zechariah falters. His question—*How shall I know this?*—reveals a heart worn thin by waiting. This is their mistake, and it is deeply human. Faithfulness over time does not exempt us from doubt. Zechariah's disbelief does not cancel the promise, but it does delay his voice.

Elizabeth's response contrasts beautifully. When she conceives, she does not rush into public celebration. She withdraws, treasuring the miracle privately. Her gratitude is not loud; it is reverent. She recognizes that God has removed her reproach, but she also understands that some blessings need time to settle into the soul before they are shared. This reveals another feature of their relationship: *mutual reverence for God's work, even when experienced differently*.

Zechariah's silence becomes a quiet discipline. Unable to speak, he listens. He watches Elizabeth carry the promise he once doubted. In this season, love is refined. Elizabeth does not belittle him. She does not weaponize his moment of weakness. Instead, she continues to walk beside him with dignity. Their relationship teaches us that correction does not require contempt, and that grace within marriage allows room for growth.

When the time comes for the child to be named, Zechariah and Elizabeth stand united. Despite pressure to follow tradition, they choose obedience. The child will be called John. In this moment, Zechariah's voice returns—not just physically, but spiritually. His praise pours out, prophetic and powerful. Doubt gives way to declaration. Silence gives way to song.

John's anointing does not arrive in spite of his parents' righteousness, but through it. Zechariah and Elizabeth do not merely produce a child—they steward a calling. Their home becomes the first classroom for the one who will prepare the way for the Lord. Their discipline, humility, and devotion shape a man whose voice will shake nations.

The lessons of their love story are enduring.

First, faithfulness is not wasted, even when it feels unseen. Zechariah and Elizabeth lived righteously long before the miracle arrived. God honored their obedience in His time.

Second, doubt does not disqualify, but it does require correction. Zechariah's silence was not punishment—it was preparation.

Third, love rooted in shared faith can carry disappointment without breaking. Elizabeth's patience and Zechariah's perseverance kept their marriage whole when many would have grown bitter.

Finally, their story teaches us that God often entrusts great purpose to those who have learned to wait well. Anointed outcomes are frequently born in quiet homes where obedience is ordinary.

Zechariah and Elizabeth show us that love does not need applause to be powerful. Their relationship reminds us that righteousness practiced in private can change public history—and that sometimes, the greatest voices are born from long seasons of silence.

------------------------------------------------------------------

## Zechariah and Elizabeth in the Modern World

If Zechariah and Elizabeth were living in the modern world, their marriage would likely be described as steady, principled, and quietly faithful—admirable, though often overlooked. They would not be influencers or trendsetters, but the kind of couple whose consistency anchors a community. Their lives would be marked more by service than by spectacle, more by integrity than by attention. In a culture that celebrates visibility, they would embody faithfulness without applause.

Zechariah would be a man devoted to his calling—perhaps a pastor, chaplain, or community leader—respected for his reliability rather than his charisma. He would believe deeply in God, yet carry the fatigue that comes from praying the same prayer for many years without an answer. In the modern world, his moment of doubt would look familiar: asking for evidence, reassurance, or timelines in an age conditioned by data and immediacy. His silence, then, would resemble a season of inward reflection—learning again how to listen more than speak.

Elizabeth would be a woman of quiet strength, navigating infertility or delayed fulfillment with dignity in a world saturated with comparison. Baby announcements, social media milestones, and unspoken expectations would intensify her grief, yet she would not allow it to harden her heart. She would likely find solace in prayer, trusted friendships, and service. Her faith would not be loud, but it would be resilient—capable of holding both sorrow and hope at once.

Together, Zechariah and Elizabeth would model a marriage rooted in shared values rather than shared outcomes. They would seek counseling or spiritual guidance not because their relationship is failing, but because they value alignment. When the long-awaited blessing finally arrives, they would receive it with humility, understanding that faithfulness precedes fulfillment.

In the modern world, Zechariah and Elizabeth would remind us that righteous living still matters, that waiting is not wasted, and that some of the greatest purposes are entrusted to those who learn how to remain faithful in silence.

# 15

# Christ and the Church

## *Love That Pursues, Covers, and Perfects*

Some love stories are written in moments. Others are written across generations. The love story of Christ and the Church is written across eternity. It is not born of convenience, chemistry, or compatibility, but of covenant—one sealed with blood, sustained by mercy, and perfected through sacrifice. This relationship is not merely theological language or religious metaphor; it is the most intimate and demanding picture of love Scripture offers. It is also the clearest blueprint for how a husband is meant to love his wife and how a wife is meant to respond to her husband.

From the beginning, Scripture frames God's relationship with His people in relational terms—bridegroom and bride, shepherd and flock, father and children. But in Christ, the imagery deepens. Love takes on flesh. Pursuit becomes personal. And covenant moves from tablets of stone to the human heart.

The Church is not portrayed as perfect when Christ loves her. She is portrayed as *chosen while broken*, *pursued while wandering*, and *cleansed while flawed*. This is the first and most uncomfortable lesson of this love story: Christ does not wait for perfection before He commits—He commits in order to perfect.

"But God commendeth his love toward us, in that, while we were yet sinners, Christ died for us."
—Romans 5:8

Christ's love is initiating love. The Church does not first reach upward; He reaches down. He chooses. He calls. He gives Himself. This is not mutual attraction—it is sacrificial pursuit. And this sets the standard for husbands.

**The Husband's Role: Love That Lays Down Its Life**

Paul makes the analogy unmistakably clear:

"Husbands, love your wives, even as Christ also loved the church, and gave himself for it."
—Ephesians 5:25

This is not romantic language. It is cruciform language. The model for a husband is not dominance, control, or entitlement—it is *self-giving*. Christ's love is active, protective, and costly. He does not rule the Church by fear; He leads her by sacrifice.

Christ covers the Church. When she is exposed in her sin, He does not discard her—He redeems her.

"That he might sanctify and cleanse it with the washing of water by the word."
—Ephesians 5:26

This is a love that washes, not shames. Corrects, not condemns. A husband, in this pattern, is meant to be a covering—not a critic, not a tyrant, not a passive bystander. He is responsible for the spiritual atmosphere of the home, just as Christ tends the spiritual life of the Church.

Christ does not exploit weakness. He strengthens it.

"For we have not an high priest which cannot be touched with the feeling of our infirmities."
—Hebrews 4:15

This tenderness matters. Authority without compassion becomes abuse. Leadership without empathy becomes tyranny. Christ's headship is gentle, intentional, and deeply personal. He knows the Church's failures, yet He remains faithful.

This reveals a critical lesson for husbands: love is proven not by control, but by consistency.

**The Wife's Role: Trust That Responds, Honors, and Aligns**

The Church's role in this relationship is not silence or erasure—it is *responsive trust*. Paul writes:

"Therefore as the church is subject unto Christ, so let the wives be to their own husbands in every thing."
—Ephesians 5:24

This verse has often been misused, stripped of context, and weaponized. But in the full analogy, submission is not subjugation—it is *alignment*. The Church submits to Christ because He is trustworthy. His commands are rooted in love. His authority is exercised for her good.

Submission, in this sense, is not weakness—it is confidence that leadership will not harm.

The Church responds to Christ's love with loyalty. She is called to faithfulness, not perfection.

"Let us be glad and rejoice, and give honour to him: for the marriage of the Lamb is come, and his wife hath made herself ready."
—Revelation 19:7

Notice the language: *made herself ready*. The Church is not passive. She grows, prepares, repents, and matures. Her obedience is not coerced; it is chosen.

This reveals the lesson for wives: honor grows where trust is cultivated, not demanded. Just as the Church learns to rely on Christ through His proven faithfulness, a wife's response flows most naturally where love is safe and sacrificial.

**The Mistake in the Relationship: Unfaithfulness and Forgetfulness**

The Bible is honest about the Church's failures. She wanders. She compromises. She forgets her first love.

"Nevertheless I have somewhat against thee, because thou hast left thy first love."
—Revelation 2:4

This is the central fracture in the relationship—not Christ's failure, but the Church's distraction. She chases substitutes. She entertains idols. She grows lukewarm.

"I know thy works, that thou art neither cold nor hot."
—Revelation 3:15

Yet Christ's response is not abandonment—it is correction and pursuit.

"As many as I love, I rebuke and chasten: be zealous therefore, and repent."
—Revelation 3:19

This is love that disciplines without discarding. Love that confronts without cancelling. And this, too, instructs marriage. Correction without cruelty. Accountability without rejection.

**Redemption and Reunion: Love That Finishes What It Starts**

The love story of Christ and the Church does not end in struggle—it ends in union.

"And I heard as it were the voice of a great multitude... saying, Alleluia: for the Lord God omnipotent reigneth."
—Revelation 19:6

Christ returns not as a distant Savior, but as a Bridegroom.

"And the Spirit and the bride say, Come."
—Revelation 22:17

This final image matters. Love is consummated. Covenant is fulfilled. The pursuit that began at the cross ends in communion.

For marriage, this means love must be long-sighted. It must endure seasons of growth, failure, correction, and renewal. Husbands are called to love with patience. Wives are called to respond with faith. Both are called to humility.

**The Ultimate Lesson**

The love story of Christ and the Church teaches us this: Love is not sustained by emotion—it is sustained by covenant.

Christ shows husbands how to lead without crushing, how to love without withdrawing, how to sacrifice without resenting. The Church shows wives how to trust without disappearing, how to follow without losing identity, how to honor without fear.

Together, they reveal God's design for love—not domination, not rivalry, not convenience—but unity forged through truth, sacrifice, and grace.

And in that design, love does not merely survive. It *redeems*.

--------------------------------------------------------------

**Christ and the Church in the Modern World**

In the modern world, the relationship between Christ and the Church is often spoken of, but rarely *lived*. It is discussed in sermons, debated in doctrine, and reduced to weekly gatherings, yet the biblical vision is far more demanding—and far more beautiful. The Church was never meant to be a religious institution competing for relevance. It was meant to be a *living body*, shaped by obedience, united by covenant, and governed by the ways of Christ Himself. Not a lifestyle accessory. A lifestyle.

From the beginning, Christ did not call people to religion; He called them to *follow*. To walk as He walked. To live differently in the midst of a broken world. The Church, therefore, is not defined by buildings, denominations, or cultural alignment, but by imitation. "If ye love me, keep my commandments" (John 14:15) was not a poetic suggestion—it was the framework of relationship. Love for Christ is demonstrated through obedience, not sentiment.

In the modern age, the Church has often settled for belief without embodiment. Faith is professed, but the commandments are treated as optional or outdated. Yet Scripture never separates love from obedience, nor grace from responsibility. Christ did not abolish righteous living; He fulfilled it and taught His people how to walk it from the heart. A Church aligned with Christ does not ask how close it can get to the world without consequence, but how fully it can reflect the character of its King.

This is why the Church must be understood as a *holy nation*, not a spiritual club. Peter writes, "But ye are a chosen generation, a royal priesthood, an holy nation, a peculiar people" (1 Peter 2:9). A nation has culture, economy, law, shared values, and mutual responsibility. The Church was meant to function the same way—God's people living under God's rule, governed by God's ways, regardless of where they are physically scattered.

In the modern world, this means the Church cannot live fragmented lives—holy on one day, indistinguishable the rest of the week. Christ is not Lord of Sundays only. He is Lord of business, family, money, speech, relationships, and ethics. The early believers understood this. They ate together, worked together, supported one another financially, and shared responsibility for the wellbeing of the body. Their faith shaped how they traded, how they governed disputes, and how they treated the vulnerable.

A Church aligned with Christ today must recover this unity of life. Business should not be separate from faith. Fellowship should not be shallow. Charity should not be occasional. The body of Christ is meant to function as one organism—each member supplying what the other lacks. When one rises, all benefit. When one falls, all respond. This is not socialism or ideology—it is covenant living.

Paul describes this clearly: "Now ye are the body of Christ, and members in particular" (1 Corinthians 12:27). A body does not compete with itself. It does not abandon injured parts. It does not elevate one function while neglecting another. Yet in the modern Church, fragmentation has become normalized— divided by politics, class, nationality, and personal ambition. Christ did not die to create rival factions. He died to create *one body*.

Loyalty, then, becomes a defining issue. The Church cannot serve multiple masters. Christ made this plain. Allegiance to Him must outweigh allegiance to nations, political systems, ideologies, or principalities. This does not mean believers disengage from society; it means their ultimate identity is not derived from it. The Church is first loyal to Christ's kingdom,

Christ's commandments, and Christ's mission. Earthly affiliations are temporary. Covenant is eternal.

This loyalty demands courage in the modern world. It means refusing to bend Christ's teachings to fit cultural pressure. It means speaking truth with humility, living set apart without arrogance, and choosing obedience even when it costs comfort or popularity. The Church must remember that it is not called to be liked—it is called to be faithful.

To live this way is to return to the original design: Christ as head, the Church as His body, moving in harmony. Christ leads through sacrifice, truth, and righteousness. The Church responds through obedience, unity, and faithful action. This relationship is not maintained through ritual alone, but through daily practice—loving God, loving one another, keeping His commandments, and building a shared life that reflects heaven's order on earth.

In the modern world, a Church that lives this way would stand out—not because it is loud, but because it is *whole*. Not because it is perfect, but because it is aligned. A people walking together. A holy nation in practice, not just in name. Loyal to Christ above all.

# About the Author

Karajah Yashar is a writer, teacher, and publisher focused on restoring biblical understanding, covenant living, and purpose-driven relationships through Scripture-centered writing. As the founder of **Passed Over Press** and its associated imprints, he develops books and study resources that challenge modern religious assumptions while calling readers back to the Bible's original intent—as a guide for life, community, and identity.

His work explores themes of love, obedience, restoration, and nation-building, bridging ancient Scripture with modern realities. Known for a clear, thoughtful, and uncompromising voice, Karajah writes to equip individuals and families to live out their faith as a lifestyle rather than a tradition.